Football Skills

By James Edward

Character illustrations by Jon Stuart

READ

All over the world people love playing football. It is the most popular game in the world.

You can play it almost anywhere, and it's a great way to make friends.

This book gives you tips to help you improve your game.

TALK

- Ask children if they play football at school or with friends.
- Do they support a football team? If 'yes', which one?
- Have they ever gone to watch a football match or seen one on TV?

ACTIVITY

- Remind children that the letter *a* in ball makes the /or/ sound (i.e. as in *all*).

Tip

See the inside back cover for more guidance on sounds.

All you need is a ball!

Kicking the ball

READ

Kicking the ball in the right direction is one of the most important skills you have to practise when learning to play football. It means that you can pass to your teammates, dribble round defenders and score goals!

1 It is easier to aim the ball if you use the inside of your foot to kick it.

2 Kick about halfway down the ball to make it go in a straight line.

3 Kick the ball near the bottom to make it go up in the air.

1

Be sure to kick with this part of the foot.

ACTIVITY

- **Have some fun!** Next time the children are outdoors playing football, encourage them to use the side of their foot to kick the ball. Can they make it go up in the air?

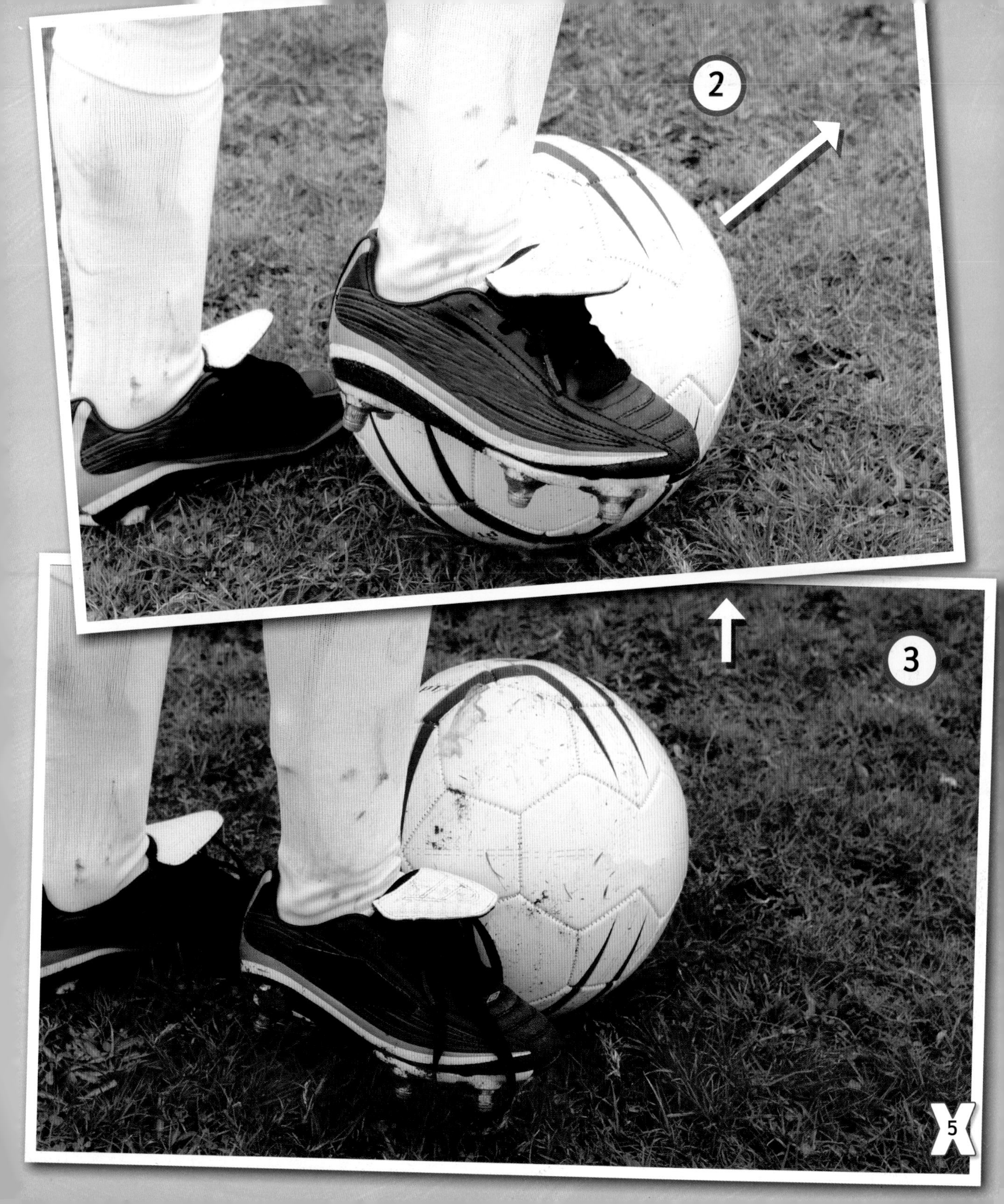
2
3

Ball control

READ

You need to be able to keep control of the ball during a match.

1 Practise dropping the ball then kicking it back up gently with the top of your foot.

How many times can you kick it up without dropping it?

2 Now practise keeping the ball up in the air using your knees.

1

ACTIVITY

- Read out the following sentence, and ask children to say the missing words: *The girl and boy are … in one place and … the balls on to their knees.* (clue: the words have the same ending as *keeping*). (standing, dropping)
- **Have some fun!** Next time the children are outdoors playing football, get them to count how many times they can kick a football up with their foot or knee.

2

They are keeping the ball up in the air.

Running with the ball

READ

It is useful to practise dribbling (running) with the ball.

1 Run forward and gently tap the ball with the inside of your foot.

2 Then tap the ball with the outside of your foot.

Use both feet. Keep the ball just in front of you.

ACTIVITY

- Ask children to look at the main picture. Then read out the following sentence: *He looks down at the ball.*
- Ask children to write the sentence. Children could use magnetic letters, a whiteboard or a pencil and paper to write.
- **Have some fun!** Next time the children are outdoors playing football, ask them to practise dribbling.

Now you can shoot or kick the ball to a pal.

Passing the ball

READ

Football is a team game and you must pass the ball to other players to help your team win.*

1 Turn your body a little to the side and aim carefully.

Kick the middle of the ball with the inside of your foot.

2 If you want to make the ball go further, let your leg swing back before you kick it.

ACTIVITY

- Ask children to write the words *near*, *goal* and *shoot*. Then ask them to put sound buttons under the words (i.e. **near**, **goal**, **shoot**).
- **Have some fun!** Next time the children are outdoors playing football, get them to practise passing the ball to each other.

She can pass the ball back to her pal.

* The /a/ sound in the word *pass* will vary according to accent.

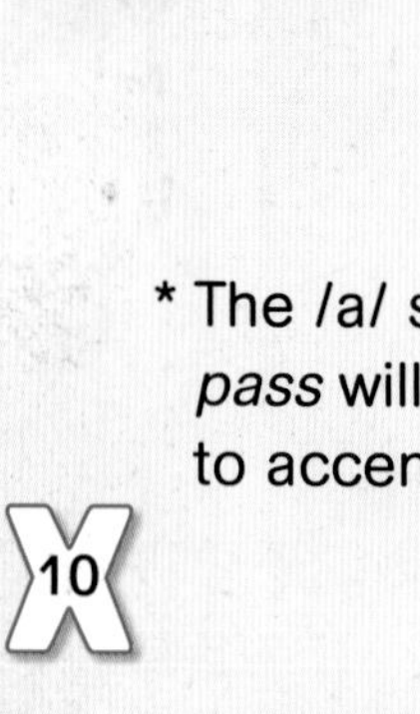

2

Now he is nearer to the goal. He can shoot!

Stopping the ball

READ

During a game, you may need to stop the ball. This may be because you want to get it under control, or so you can take the time to look around and work out where to pass it.

1 When the ball comes towards you, move your foot backwards as the ball hits it. This will cushion the ball and stop it from bouncing off your foot.

2 Another way to stop the ball is to trap it. Lift your foot and trap the ball under your heel.

TALK

- Talk about how Tiger is stopping the ball.
- Ask the children to look at the picture. What time of year is it? How do you think the children will keep warm?

She stops the ball with her heel.

Shooting at goal

READ

The aim of the game is for your team to score as many goals as possible.

It is useful to practise scoring when the ball is moving. Ask a friend to pass the ball to you so that you can have a go.

Run forward to the ball and kick it with the side of your foot. Aim the ball away from the goalkeeper.

ACTIVITY

- Read out the following sentence, and ask children to say missing word: *She will ... the ball go 'thud' into the back of the net.* (clue: it rhymes with *near*). (hear)
- Ask children to write the word *hear*.
- **Have some fun!** Next time the children are outdoors playing football, get them to practise shooting at the goal.

She is near the goal. She swings her foot and kicks the ball hard.

All join in!

READ

Now you know some basic football skills. There are many others that you will learn as you play.

The most important thing is that you have fun playing.

Good luck, play fair and have a great game!

TALK

- Talk about passing. Ask children how they know who to pass the ball to.
- Talk about why games have rules.

Pass to me!

Now you can join in the fun!